Dinosaurs?

Story by Mike Graf

Illustrations by Warwick Bennett

BEN AND JODIE
ALMOST DIED HERE
OCT. 2004.

Rigby PM Plus Chapter Books
part of the Rigby PM Program
Sapphire Level

Published by Harcourt Achieve Inc.
10801 N. MoPac Expressway
Building #3
Austin, TX 78759
www.harcourtachieve.com

10 9 8 7 6 5
07 06

Printed in China by 1010 Printing International Ltd

Dinosaurs?
ISBN 0 75786 936 X

Contents

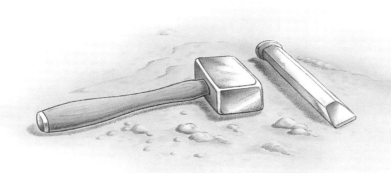

Chapter 1

Flash Flood

"I knew we shouldn't have come down into the canyon!" Jodie said, her hair soaking.

Ben stuck his hand out in the pouring rain. "At least it's not snowing!" He shivered and wrapped his arms around his body.

Jodie and Ben huddled against the side of the cliff, protected from the rain by an overhanging shelf of rock above them. Wind whipped trees around and blew sheets of rain furiously across the canyon.

Jodie turned to Ben. "We have to be home before dark, and we've got miles to cover."

"I know," Ben replied. "I'll go check the sky." He jumped outside. The drenching rain instantly soaked him. The sky was dark gray, but off to the west, the sun peeked out of the clouds. "I think it's going to clear soon," Ben announced, dashing back to shelter.

"Let's make a run for it," Jodie said.

They bolted outside and onto the wet trail, which quickly led them to a raging, muddy stream.

"We'll have to jump," Ben concluded.

"This is definitely the last time I go exploring with you," Jodie replied.

They backed up a few steps. "One, two, three ... jump!" they counted together.

Thump! Jodie made it to the other side, but saw Ben plunge into water up to his waist. Ben tried to grasp a rock at the side of the creek. "I can't hold on!" he shouted, as the rapidly flowing water began to pull him downstream.

Jodie reached behind her and grabbed onto a tree root. She held out her leg. "Grab my foot!"

Ben took hold of both of Jodie's feet, but his weight pulled her closer to the raging water.

"Hang on!" Jodie screamed, and gripped the slippery tree root with both hands while Ben struggled toward shallower water. "Okay!" he gasped.

Ben clambered onto the stream bank, his shoes dragging. He wiped his muddy face, looked at Jodie, and grinned. "That was fun!"

Jodie rolled her eyes. "Let's go." They headed down the trail toward their mountain bikes and home.

Chapter 2
Return to the Canyon

"So you're saying, Jodie, that you left your homework in a cave?" Mr. Block questioned his sixth-grade student.

"Sort of a cave," Jodie gulped, looking across at Ben. Ben smiled. Mr. Block looked at both his students. "I'll get my homework back tonight," Jodie said. "I promise."

At the end of the day, Jodie met Ben in front of the school. "Do you want to come with me to the canyon?" Jodie asked.

"You bet," Ben replied.

Jodie and Ben hid their bikes in some bushes and walked along the faint path that they followed yesterday. At the top of a hill, they scanned the terrain spread out below.

Ben pointed ahead. "There's the cave."

Jodie and Ben hiked on. Finally the path cut downward, weaving its way alongside layers of red and green rock. With one last effort, they scurried up the hillside and into the cave.

Jodie picked up her backpack and unzipped it. "Phew!" she sighed. "My books are dry." Slipping her backpack on, she said, "I'd better get back and start that homework."

They walked down the trail and came to the stream that Ben had fallen into. Only a trickle of water flowed along the stream's muddy bottom now. It was hard to believe it was the same one as yesterday.

Ben jumped into the streambed and stood exactly where he was almost swept away. "Look how deep the bed is," he exclaimed.

Jodie climbed down and joined him. "You definitely could have died. You were lucky."

They both walked along the stream. Rocks of all sizes and shapes jutted out of the sandy walls. Ben pried a small rock loose from the embankment and started etching in the streambed's smoothed-out wall. *Ben and Jodie almost died here. Oct. 2004.*

"Now people will know what happened to us," he announced.

"Only until it rains again," Jodie said.

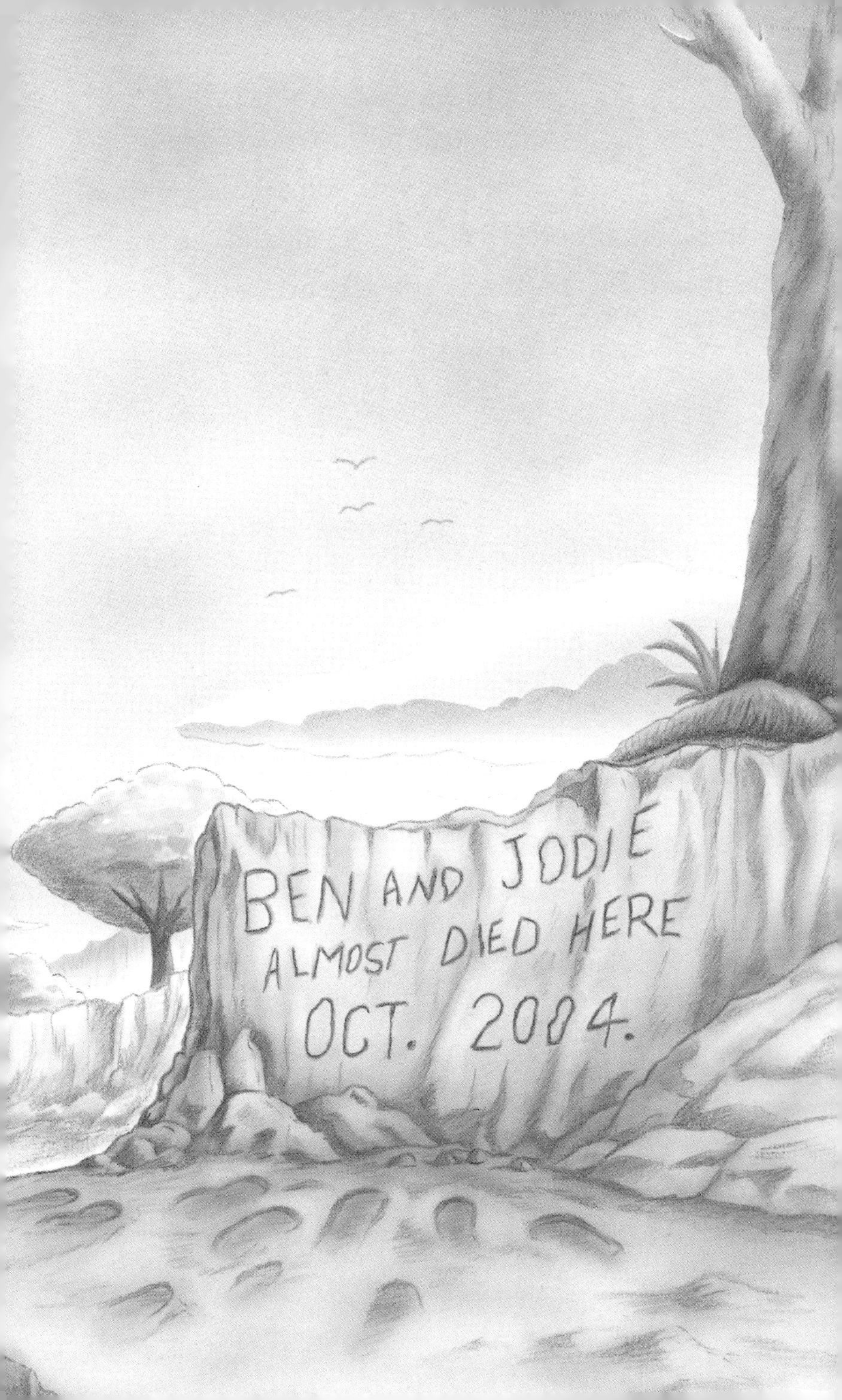
BEN AND JODIE
ALMOST DIED HERE
OCT. 2004.

Ben pulled his arm back, ready to toss the small rock into the canyon. Something stopped him. He dropped his arm down and looked at the rock again. "Hey," he whispered.

Jodie and Ben studied the small gray rock.

"It looks more like a little spool than a rock," Ben said. "A little spool of thread."

"Or a bone," Jodie added.

"It feels like ..." Ben said, weighing the rock in his hand.

"A fossilized bone?" Jodie asked.

"I bet it's from an old rat or something," Ben answered, passing the rock to Jodie.

"Yeah. Some prehistoric rat got swept away in a thunderstorm," Jodie concluded.

Jodie and Ben looked at each other with the same thought. They ran back to where Ben had pulled the rock from the cliff.

Chapter 3
A Secret Collection

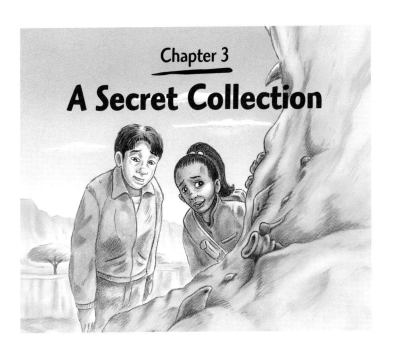

There were thousands of rocks in the sandy wall. Jodie and Ben started digging. Jodie pulled a rock out and looked at it. "This one's just a rock, I think." She tossed it away.

Jodie paused to inspect a new rock. "Here's another spool!" she called out.

Ben stepped over. "It definitely looks like an old bone," he said excitedly.

Jodie continued digging in the same place. "I think I've found another bone." She handed it carefully to Ben.

"Wait," Ben said, pulling a plastic bag out of his backpack. "Let's put what we find in here."

"Our own little collection," Jodie agreed.

Ben and Jodie put the bones in the plastic bag and searched on.

Ben dug frantically into the hillside, then stopped to inspect another rock. "Hey, look Jodie — I think it's part of a jaw!" Ben proclaimed. "Look at the tiny black teeth in it."

Jodie looked at the bone. "You can still see the sharp little grooves in the teeth. This is definitely going into our collection."

Ben and Jodie kept digging. They tossed some rocks away and put the ones that looked like bones into the bag.

Ben stopped digging. "You really think these are all bones, Jodie?"

"They're certainly shaped liked bones."

"I wonder how old they are," Ben asked.

"Or how big the rat was?" Jodie added.

"Or mouse ..."

"Or wild dog ..."

"Or dinosaur?" Jodie looked at Ben.

They both laughed, knowing dinosaurs were huge and these bones were tiny. They looked up at the late afternoon sun — time had slipped away. "I know where we're coming back tomorrow," Jodie beamed.

Ben put the bag of bones in his backpack. "Don't tell anyone. This is our secret find."

Chapter 4
Staking a Claim

"Now, don't forget. Science projects are due next week," Mr. Block reminded his students as they scurried out of the classroom at the end of the day. "There will be no excuses accepted."

Jodie and Ben stopped on the sidewalk outside school.

"Did you bring everything?" Ben asked.

"Yep," Jodie replied. "I've got plastic bags, gloves, a hammer, and a chisel."

"Me, too," Ben added.

They set off on their now-familiar trail, with only a couple of hours of daylight and digging time left.

Out of breath, they arrived at their dig site.

Jodie and Ben walked up to the small cliff where they had excavated bones the day before.

"Phew!" Jodie exclaimed. "It looks like everything is just as we left it. I was worried that someone else would come along."

"Me, too," Ben said, relieved.

Jodie and Ben jumped into the streambed and quickly started digging.

"Shh!" Jodie hissed. "Did you hear that?" It was the sound of a truck driving up the canyon.

"There are no roads up here," Ben whispered.

"Except that gated-off area," Jodie reminded him. "And that's only a dirt road."

Jodie and Ben dropped their tools, scrambled up the bank, and hid behind a tree.

The truck sounded louder. Soon it came into view. It drove along the bottom of the canyon following the main creek. Ben and Jodie could see two people in the front seat. Whatever was in the back rattled around.

"I wonder what's going on," Jodie whispered. "What are they doing here?"

Jodie and Ben watched the truck drive on until it disappeared behind some large boulders. They heard the engine turn off and doors slam shut. They continued watching, but didn't see anyone.

"Let's dig some more before it gets dark," Ben said. They climbed back into the streambed and continued their search.

The two dug and scratched until dusk. "It's past 5:00 already. We'd better get going."

Jodie and Ben put the bags of bones gently into their backpacks, happy with their discoveries.

Jodie brushed her hand over their footprints. "I don't want anyone to know we were here," she explained.

They climbed out of the creekbed and walked along the trail. When they heard voices, Jodie and Ben scurried up a large sandstone rock and peered over the edge.

Three people were putting equipment in the truck, next to a second vehicle. They loaded up picks, shovels, a wheelbarrow, and what looked like a bucket of rocks.

"We'll dig again tomorrow," one person said. "This is quite a lucky break."

The three people got back into the vehicles, turned them around, and drove off.

Jodie and Ben watched them disappear down the dirt road. Ben jumped up. "Let's go down there and check it out."

"We can't!" Jodie frowned. "Footprints, Ben. It will be too dark to clear our footprints if we go down there now."

Chapter 5

String, Shovels, and Brushes

"So, Jodie. Have you thought about your science project yet?" Mr. Block asked.

"Uh, yes," Jodie replied. "I think I'll do it on weather. Or something."

"Weather?" Mr. Block asked with interest.

"Mm, thunderstorms and sunshine and stuff." Jodie held up a book on weather patterns.

"Well, Jodie, remember it is due on Monday," Mr. Block spoke.

At last, the bell rang.

Jodie and Ben dashed out the door. They raced their bikes on the whole trail, their heavy backpacks jingling with equipment.

They got to their spot in record time. Quickly, Jodie and Ben started pulling out and examining rocks, saving only the ones that looked like bones.

Then they heard the "chink" of metal and low voices talking.

Jodie and Ben put down their tools, got out of the streambed, and climbed up the same rock as yesterday to investigate.

The three people and the trucks were there again. One man was measuring the area and hammering stakes into the ground. A woman dusted off rocks with a brush, and a second man was working with a spade.

"If they are buried in this layer of soil, they've got to be at least 100 million years old," one of the men said.

"This could be one of the best paleontological finds here in years," the woman said. "It's fantastic."

"It could take us months to get this femur and some of the other large bones out," the man with the shovel added.

Jodie and Ben looked at each other, amazed. "Dinosaurs!"

They turned to watch the paleontologists.

"I wonder what else we'll find out here," the woman with the brush said.

Another paleontologist let his measuring tape reel back in. "We might find baby dinosaur fossils. There might be several different types of dinosaurs here."

The paleontologists kept on with their work. Jodie and Ben watched them from above.

The paleontologist with the brush stood up and called out to the others. "Hey! Take a look at these tiny bones."

The scientists gathered around a rock. The trio seemed very excited about something.

Jodie and Ben looked at each other, then climbed down the side of the rock and onto the trail.

They walked up to the paleontologists.

"Excuse me," Jodie spoke.

The scientists quickly turned around.

"We've found something we'd like you to look at," Ben said.

"Yeah," Jodie added. "We were out here the other day during the storm. We found all these tiny rocks or maybe bones."

"We think they're from a rat or something."

"At least, we thought they were."

"You two were out here during that storm?" one of the men asked.

"Yes," Ben answered, then looked at Jodie. "We were just exploring after school."

"Good timing. The best time to dig is right after a storm," the other said. "The rain washes away the topsoil, and the bones are uncovered."

"Can we see the bones?" the woman asked.

"Sure," Jodie answered. "But some are at home. This is our fourth day out here."

Jodie and Ben led the paleontologists up to the gully, then down into the streambed.

Ben took a handful of tiny rocks from their collection and showed them to the paleontologists. They passed them around.

"Where did you find these?" one asked.

"It's unbelievable how tiny they are," another added. "And in such good condition."

"They may be from unborn baby dinosaurs. I wonder if there are any eggshell pieces around," the third person said.

Ben pointed to the streambed. "We've been pulling all of these out of here."

"Do you realize what these actually are?" one of the scientists asked.

Ben and Jodie shrugged their shoulders.

"We thought they were from a rat or something," Jodie replied.

"Not at all," a paleontologist explained. "Quite likely they are baby Dryosaurus bones. When fully grown, they were about five feet tall and about 10 feet long."

"They looked a bit like birds, with a small head," the scientist went on, "and had grinding teeth for eating plants. We just pulled a nearly complete Dryosaurus skull from the ground yesterday. We hope there may be other sorts of dinosaurs here, too."

Jodie and Ben looked at each other, their eyes wide. "We've discovered dinosaur bones!"

"It certainly looks that way," one of the scientists said. "Can we see the rest of your collection?"

"Sure," Jodie and Ben answered.

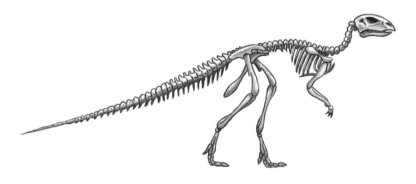

Chapter 6
A Top Project

Mr. Block and the whole class stood high above the stream. Ben and Jodie pointed down into the gully at the three paleontologists, who were busy measuring out the new dig site.

Jodie explained, "This whole area is part of the Morrison Formation, which is rich in fossilized dinosaur bones. The bones are over 100 million years old. But not all of them are big — we learned that." Jodie looked at Ben.

"We found lots of tiny fossils that look like spools of thread. They are vertebrae, or parts of a dinosaur's backbone." Jodie carefully held up several small bones. "If you'd like to climb down into the streambed, we can introduce you to baby Dryosaurus fossils."

The class clambered down to the site. While the students talked excitedly with the scientists, Mr. Block said, "Very impressive, Jodie. I certainly didn't expect all of this!"

Jodie looked at her teacher. "I couldn't have done it without Ben."

Mr. Block asked, "But didn't you say your project was going to be about weather?"

"Well, it sort of started with weather," Jodie smiled, then glanced at Ben.